Girls' Crafts

Tips & Techniques
for Fabulous Fun!

Mud Puddle Books
NEW YORK

Girls' Crafts:
Tips & Techniques for Fabulous Fun

ISBN: 978-1-60311-205-5

The material in this book has previously appeared in slightly different form.
For a complete list of credits and copyright information, please see page 128.

Published in 2009 by:
Mud Puddle Books
54 W. 21st Street
Suite 601
New York, NY 10010
info@mudpuddlebooks.com

Printed in China

Contents

introduction

Girls' Crafts **will introduce you to a wide range of craft ideas that are both fabulous and fun. Tips and techniques are easy to follow, and the results are sensational. Craft projects are ideal when you want some alone time, but they are just as wonderful to do with friends.**

Beaded Friendship Bracelets

Friendship bracelets are a way of saying "you're special to me" that is much more meaningful than something store-bought. You can make unique bracelets that are casual or dressy and suited for any occasion.

Hair Wraps: All the Things You Need to Know for Easy and Beautiful Hair Decoration

Today, women of all ages wrap their hair, whether it's short or long, braided or loose. Hair wraps can be considered another piece of jewelry and are colorful, festive, fun, vibrant, cool, elegant, subtle, sophisticated, glamorous and just plain pretty.

Fancy Feet: A Treat for Your Feet!

Beautiful feet, like beautiful hands, can really get you noticed. They deserve to be pampered with soothing pedicures and foot massages. You can brighten them with an enormous range of colorful decorations that are sure to catch everyone's eye. Most of all, fancy feet are fun!

Let's Make Clothespin Dolls

The making of clothespin dolls is as much fun today as it was in a time before department stores and mass merchandisers. Using scraps of fabric, paper and ribbon, you can transform ordinary clothespins into extraordinary dolls.

Painting on Rocks
Painting Animals on Rocks

Rock painting is an easy and inexpensive way to create your own art, and painted rocks make unique and expressive indoor or outdoor decorations.
And, they make wonderful gifts!

Beaded Friendship Bracelets

by Kaylee Connor

INTRODUCTION

What exactly is a friend? Webster's dictionary defines friend "as someone who is not an enemy." To us, friends can be classmates, roommates, companions, confidantes, soul mates, allies, collaborators, teammates, peers, or supporters. A friend is a person that helps you, encourages you, questions you when she is in doubt, has fun with you, works with you, stands by you when you need her, and finally, needs you as much as you need her. A friend can be a casual friend, a good friend, a close friend, or your very best friend.

A friend is a person you want to do something nice for, whether it's a special occasion like her birthday, or just because it's Tuesday and you feel like it. A friend is a person that you want to thank in a "you're special to me" sort of handmade way.

That is why making friendship bracelets—for a friend or with a friend—is so much more meaningful than something store-bought. It's a special gift that you made with her in mind, something just for her. Remember, if it is made by hand, it comes from the heart.

Friendship bracelets are easy, fun, and inexpensive. You can make one or one hundred! Making unique bracelets for any occasion is simple—make them casual or dressy; beaded or plain; or from thread, ribbons, or strips of fabric. Your imagination is all you need to be a designer *extraordinaire* of friendship bracelets.

THREAD OR FLOSS:

Traditional six-strand embroidery thread, usually called embroidery floss, is most often used to make friendship bracelets.

SPECIALTY FIBERS:

Pearl cotton, knitting yarns, thin ribbons, soft silk-like fabrics, and specialty threads of any type can be used to make friendship bracelets.

Designer Secret:
The colors and textures of specialty fibers add a "designer touch" to even a simple project. Use them by themselves, or mix-and-match to make a variety of bracelets.

CLIPBOARD:

This book will refer to using a knotting board, but you may prefer to use a clipboard rather than cardboard and pins to hold your bracelet while you are making it. This will secure the bracelet at the top, but you will be unable to pin the knots in place as you work.

KNOTTING BOARD:

We recommend creating a knotting board by using a thick piece of cardboard—such as the side of a box—to use as a work surface for creating your friendship bracelets. The board should be firm, yet allow you to easily insert and remove pins. Use large hatpins to secure your knots in place.

TIPS

By marking the end length of your bracelet on the knotting board or clipboard, you will know at a glance just how long the bracelet needs to be.

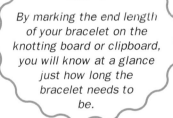

BEADS:

Beads of any type and size can be used to embellish your friendship bracelets. You will want to make certain that the thread or fiber you are using will fit through the hole of the bead. If you have difficulty getting the thread through the bead hole, you can use a beading wire loop (see page 12) to help you. If the bead hole is just too small, try adding a length of thin, 24-gauge wire to your threads. The beads will easily slip onto the wire.

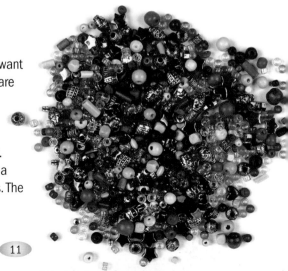

BEADING WIRE LOOP:

This loop is optional, but can make it easier to add beads to your bracelet. Simply take a thin piece of 24-gauge wire, bend, and wrap as show in diagram.

EMBELLISHMENTS:

Almost anything can be used to adorn friendship bracelets. Charms for jewelry-making, small craft items such as miniature Christmas garlands, or a multitude of scrapbooking embellishments can be added. Walk up and down the aisles of your favorite fabric or craft store and see all of the wonderful things that can be used.

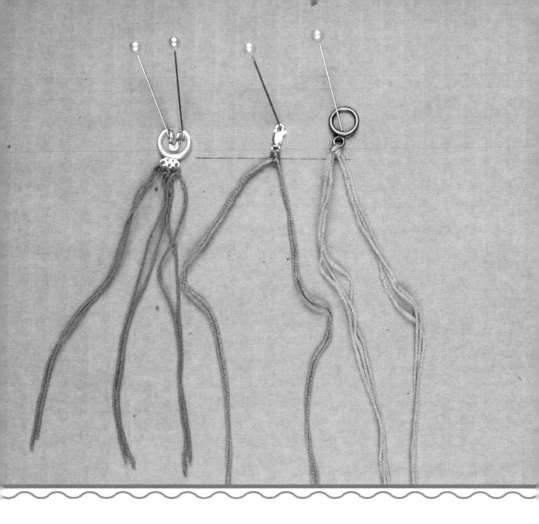

JEWELRY CLOSURES:

Jewelry closures are optional; however, they make removing your friendship bracelet a snap! See Ending Your Bracelet on page 18.

MISCELLANEOUS TOOLS AND MATERIALS:

24-Gauge Beading Wire
Fabric Glue
Ruler
Scissors

BASIC KNOTS

There are 3 basic knots used to make friendship bracelets in this book. They are easy to master and easy to remember, but you may want to practice a little before beginning to make your first friendship bracelet. A little practice now will save a considerable amount of frustration, time, and materials.

OVERHAND KNOTS

This knot can be created with as few as 2 threads, but you can use as many threads as you like.

Right Overhand Knot
Step 1

Measure at least 2 threads to be 4 times the length of the finished bracelet. (Double the length if you will be folding the threads in half before you start knotting.)

Tightly hold the left-hand thread and knot the remaining thread around it.

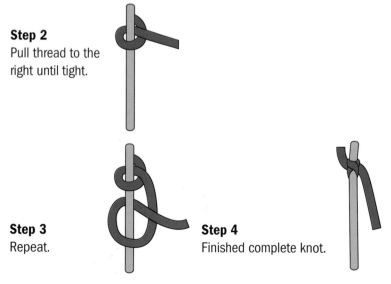

Step 2
Pull thread to the right until tight.

Step 3
Repeat.

Step 4
Finished complete knot.

Left Overhand Knot
Step 1
Measure at least 2 threads to be 4 times the length of the finished bracelet. (Double the length if you will be folding the threads in half before you start knotting.)

Tightly hold the right-hand thread and knot the remaining thread around it.

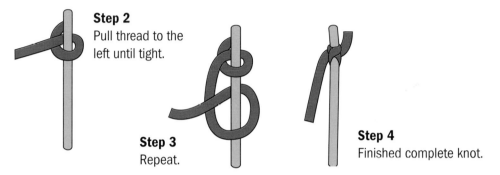

Step 2
Pull thread to the left until tight.

Step 3
Repeat.

Step 4
Finished complete knot.

Notes:
1. In this book the overhand knot is sometimes completed as a right overhand knot and sometimes as a left overhand knot, but either way it is the same knot.
2. The overhand knot can be made with as many threads as you want.

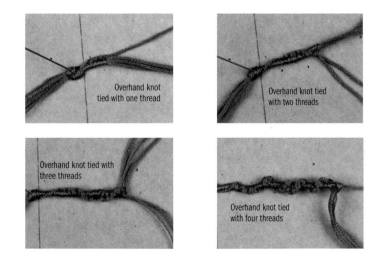

Overhand knot tied with one thread

Overhand knot tied with two threads

Overhand knot tied with three threads

Overhand knot tied with four threads

SQUARE KNOT

Step 1

Measure each of 4 strands to be 4 times the desired length of the finished bracelet. Knot the strands together at one end, and pin the knot to the knotting board. Separate the strands.

Step 2

Move thread #4 from the far right and cross it over the center threads (#2 and #3) and under thread #1.

Step 3

Move thread #1 over thread #4 and under threads #2 and #3.

Step 4

Bring thread #1 from behind through the loop in thread #4 (far right).

Step 5

Pull on threads #1 and #4 to create the first half of the square knot.

Step 6

Move thread #4 from the left and cross it over the center strands (#2 and #3) and under thread #1.

Step 7

Bring thread #1 under threads #2 and #3 and through the loop on the far left.

Step 8

Pull on threads #1 and #4 to finish the square knot.

ENDING YOUR BRACELET

Each of the projects in this book tells how to end the bracelet as it is pictured in the example. However, the following endings can be used with any of the bracelets you learn to make, so feel free to make any substitutions.

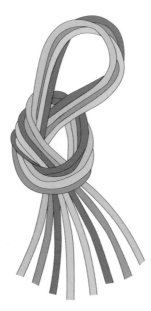

POSSIBILITY 1: LOOPED-END BRACELET

Folding the threads in half when starting the bracelet will create a loop at one end that can be used for tying bracelet ends together.

To Wear:
Wrap the finished bracelet around your wrist. Divide the threads at the loose end, and slip one half the threads through the loop. Tie to the other half of the threads, securing in a double knot so that the bracelet does not come untied.

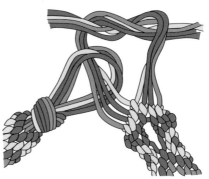

POSSIBILITY 2: LOOSE-ENDS BRACELET

This bracelet is made by using single strands of thread that are not folded in half and looped.

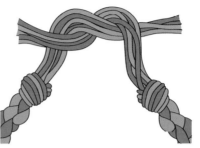

To Wear:

Wrap the finished bracelet around your wrist. Tie ends together in a double knot, cutting longer ends to desired length.

POSSIBILITY 3: JEWELRY CLOSURE BRACELET

These bracelets have jewelry closures at both ends just like traditional jewelry, making it possible to remove the bracelet as often as desired.

The closures are easiest to attach when the bracelet is made from 3 or 4 strands of embroidery floss. After tying the closures to the bracelet ends, you may need to place a small amount of fabric glue over the knots to keep them secure.

To Wear:

Attach this bracelet to your wrist just as you would attach any piece of traditional jewelry.

TIPS

Fastening your bracelets with Possibility 1 or Possibility 2 is best for those that will be worn until you tire of them. Tying and untying the threads will eventually fray them, making it difficult to tie a secure knot.

The projects found in this book employ fun and easy techniques. Just follow the step-by-step instructions to create fabulous designs for you and your friends.

BASIC WRAPPED BRACELET

This easy bracelet requires a flexible core thread to wrap the threads of the bracelet around. Mix up the size of your bracelets by using a thin or thick core—and wear them singly or all together.

MATERIALS:

Core thread, thin
Embroidery floss, 1 color

STEP 1

Cut core thread to desired length of finished bracelet plus a little for finishing. Cut 2 strands of embroidery floss to 4 times the length of the core thread, tie both strands of floss to the core. Be sure to leave a long enough tail to tie your bracelet onto your wrist.

STEP 2

Pin the core thread to the knotting board. Tightly wrap both strands of floss around the core thread to the end and tie in a knot.

STEP 3

Wrap finished bracelet around wrist and tie floss ends together in a double knot. If ends are too long, trim to desired length.

WRAPPED BRACELET WITH ALTERNATING COLORS

Want to add a little variety to your wrapped bracelets? This simple bracelet alternates colors to let you and your friends show off your school colors, your club colors, or just your favorite colors.

MATERIALS:

Core thread, thin
Embroidery floss, 2 colors

STEP 1

Cut core thread to desired length of finished bracelet plus a little for finishing. Cut 2 strands of each color embroidery floss to 4 times the length of the core thread, tie all strands of floss to the core. Be sure to leave a long enough tail to tie your bracelet onto your wrist.

STEP 2

Pin the core thread to the knotting board. Tightly wrap the 2 strands of the first color of floss around the core and the second color of floss until you have the desired amount of color.

STEP 3

Pick up the strands of the second color floss and tightly wrap around both the core thread and the first color of floss until you have the desired amount of color.

STEP 4

Repeat Steps 2 and 3, alternating colors as desired until you reach the end of the core thread. Knot tightly at the end of the core thread.

STEP 5

Wrap finished bracelet around wrist and tie floss ends together in a double knot. If ends are too long, trim to desired length.

WRAPPED BRACELET WITH TWISTED THREAD

MATERIALS:

Thin cord, 1 color
Core thread, thick
Embroidery floss, 1 color

STEP 1

Cut core thread to desired
length of finished bracelet
plus a little for finishing. Cut
2 strands of embroidery floss
and 2 strands of thin cord to
4 times the length of the core
thread, tie both strands of floss
to the core. Be sure to leave
a long enough tail to tie your
bracelet onto your wrist.

STEP 2

Tie thin cord to the core thread
directly beneath the floss.

STEP 3

Pin the core thread to the Knotting
Board. Wrap the 2 embroidery floss
strands around the core thread and
thin cords for about ½" (1.3 cm).

STEP 4

Pull the thin cords up and move them out of the way. Continue wrapping core thread with embroidery floss to the end. Knot tightly at the end of the core threads.

Colored Chord

Floss

STEP 5

Twist thin cord strands together and wrap the thin cords around the floss-wrapped core. When the cord reaches the end of the solid color floss place thin cords next to core thread and wrap with floss. Tie floss and thin cords into a tight knot.

STEP 6

Wrap finished bracelet around wrist and tie floss ends together in a double knot. If ends are too long, trim to desired length.

Designer Secret:
For this variation string thin cord with beads, do not twist, wrap around wrapped core.

BASIC WRAPPED BRACELET WITH BEADS

MATERIALS:

Beads, 1 or more colors
Core thread, thin
Embroidery floss, 1 or more colors
Fabric glue (Optional)

These bracelets are made by following the steps for the Basic Wrapped Bracelet on page 20 or the Basic Wrapped Bracelet with Alternating Colors on page 22. After wrapping the core thread with the desired color(s) of floss, slip beads onto the bracelet. If beads need to be further secured into place, either secure with a dot of fabric glue or tie a piece of floss or thin ribbon on both sides of the bead or beaded section.

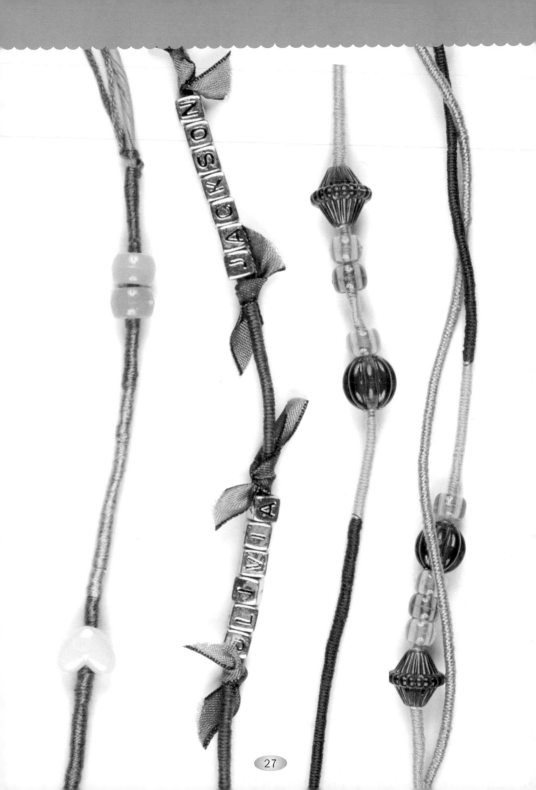

BASIC DIAGONAL STRIPE BRACELET

MATERIALS:

Embroidery floss, 4 colors

STEP 1

Measure and cut 1 strand of each color floss to 4 times the length of the finished bracelet. Tie a knot 2" (5 cm) from the top and pin to the knotting board.

STEP 2

Separate the threads.

STEP 3

Beginning with thread #1 on the far left, tie a complete overhand knot over thread #2.

STEP 4

Continuing with thread #1, make a complete overhand knot around each of the remaining threads.

Reminder: *A complete overhand knot is always tied twice.*

STEP 5

Thread #2 should now be on the far left. Begin the process again, tying complete overhand knots with thread #2 over threads #3, #4, and #1.

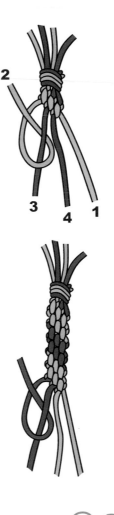

STEP 6

Continue knotting your threads in this manner until the bracelet is the desired length.

STEP 7

Tie a knot at the end of your bracelet. Trim the remaining thread to approximately 2" (5 cm).

STEP 8

Wrap finished bracelet around your wrist and tie the two knotted ends together.

TiPS

Hold each thread that is being tied straight and tight, pulling each knot you make to the same degree of snugness. This will give your finished bracelet a consistent texture.

BASIC CHEVRON BRACELET

MATERIALS:

Pearl Cotton thread, 4 colors

Note: although the Chevron Bracelet can be made with regular embroidery floss, a heavier pearl cotton will make it easier if you are just learning how to knot this design.

STEP 1

Measure 1 thread of each color to be 8 times the desired length of the finished bracelet. Fold in half and tie a knot 1" (2.54 cm) from loop. Pin to the knotting board.

STEP 2

Separate threads as shown in diagram.

STEP 3

1 2 3 4 4 3 2 1

Take the #1 thread that is on the far left and, working to the center, make a complete overhand knot onto threads #2, #3, and #4. Stop knotting and leave thread #1 in the center.

Reminder: A complete overhand knot is always tied twice.

STEP 4

Take the #1 thread that is on the far right and, working to the center, make a complete overhand knot onto threads #2, #3, and #4.

STEP 5

Tie the two middle #1 threads together using a complete overhand knot.

STEP 6

Beginning with the outermost threads and working toward the center, repeat Steps 3 to 5. Continue tying until bracelet is the desired length.

STEP 7

Tie a knot at the end of the bracelet.

STEP 8

Wrap finished bracelet around your wrist, slip the loose ends through the loop, and tie a knot.

BASIC SQUARE KNOT BRACELET WITH BEADS

MATERIALS:

Assorted beads
Embroidery floss, 1 color
Sequin strand
Thin cording

Measure and cut 3 strands embroidery floss to 8 times the desired length of finished bracelet. Fold in half and knot approximately 1" (2.54 cm) from loop. Tie a knot. Pin to the knotting board.

Following the directions for the square knot on page 12, make a series of square knots, then add 3 beads as shown. Make a second series of square knots, add 3 more beads, and finish with a final series of square knots.

Measure and cut 1 strand of thin cording and 1 strand of sequins 1½ times the desired length of finished bracelet. Holding the beaded bracelet, sequin strand, and thin cording together, knot a length of embroidery thread around one end and wrap together as shown. Repeat for other end.

Hair Wraps

*All the Fun Things You
Need to Know for Easy and
Beautiful Hair Decoration*

by Jo Packham

General Instructions

THE BASICS

Hair wrapping dates all the way back to Egypt, when kings and queens had threads of gold woven into their hair and beards. In ancient Greece, women adorned their hair with beads while women in the Middle Ages wrapped their braided hair with vibrant colored threads. Today, women of all ages wrap their hair, whether it's short or long, braided or loose. Hair wraps can be considered another "piece of" jewelry and, depending on the wrap itself, can be described in any number of words. Close your eyes and imagine a hair wrap that is colorful, festive, fun, vibrant, cool, elegant, subtle, sophisticated, sexy, or pretty. Now, open your eyes and turn the pages of this book to learn how easy it is to wrap your hair for any occasion!

Hair wraps can take anywhere from 5 to 60 minutes, depending on the complexity of the wrap. They can be temporary, lasting only for an evening or an event, or they can be created to stay in for several weeks depending on the materials you choose to work with.

The thickness of your hair wraps can depend on the amount of hair contained in the braid, the quantity and types of fibers, and the beads that you use. It's all up to you!

An endless variety of materials can be used for wrapping hair. Your imagination is the only limitation that you have.

Scissors: You will need a small pair of good quality scissors to cut your threads and fibers.

Tip: If you are using specialty fibers or embellishments, such as wire-edged ribbons or beaded trims, you will want to have two pair of scissors available: one for regular thread and one for specialty fibers and embellishments. Otherwise the wires and materials in the specialty fibers can quickly dull your scissors, resulting in ragged cuts.

Miscellaneous: You will need a brush and a comb for creating hair wraps in order to separate and detangle. A comb with a "tail" might make it easier to divide hair for braiding, but it is not essential.

Embroidery Floss: This is the most common material used for wrapping. It will stay in for the longest amount of time and is the easiest to wash while in your hair.

Tip: If you plan on keeping your wrap through several shampoos, make certain that the colors of thread you select are colorfast. Darker colors, such as red, navy blue, or black, tend to "bleed" when wet.

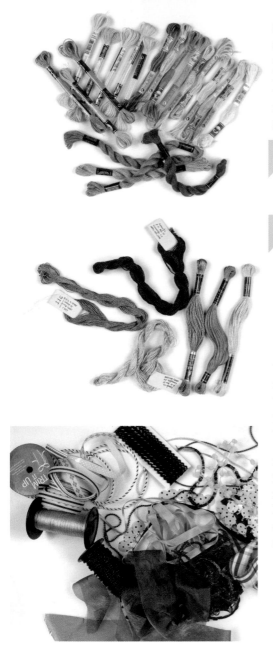

Specialty Threads: Fabric and craft stores have a large variety of fibers that can be used for hair wrapping. Metallic, variegated, or twisted cottons, as well as other fibers, can all be found in the embroidery floss section while novelty knitting yarns can also be used.

Tip: Specialty threads may be more difficult to wrap than cotton embroidery floss, but the end result is often worth the extra time and expense.

Tip: Check the strength of specialty threads before you begin to wrap. Some have thin base threads that will break easily when tension is applied. If they are too fragile for wrapping, combine the specialty thread with a strand or two of cotton floss and wrap as a unit.

Rayon Threads: Fibers that are too "slippery," such as rayon threads, might not hold the knots when wrapped into your hair. We suggest you choose a different fiber to keep your wrap secure.

Specialty Trims: Any width, print, or fiber of ribbon, seam binding, or ric rac* can be used for hair wrapping. Beaded and braided trims or strips of softer fabrics such as cotton, silk, or synthetic blends can also be used.

* Ric rac is a decorative zigzag trim.

Embellishments: Just about anything can be used to adorn your wrap. Charms for jewelry-making, small craft items such as miniature Christmas garlands, or a multitude of scrapbooking embellishments can be added to your hair wrap. Walk up and down the aisles of your favorite fabric or craft store and see all the wonderful things that can be used to adorn your hair.

Wrap Endings: A hair wrap can be ended in so many ways! The thread used to wrap the hair can be knotted at the end; a small elastic band can be used to secure the wrap in place; and beads, tassels, or other trims can be tied at the end of the wrap. Hair wraps can also be ended using a special type of hair putty found in most beauty supply stores.

Tip: Although a number of items can be used to end your wrap, make certain it is secure. You don't want your wrap to unwind or your beads to fall off!

Beads: Beads of any type or size can be used in hair wraps. However, if the bead hole is not large enough to put the hair wrap through you will have to string your beads on a separate thread or wire and attach to wrapped braid.

Beading Wire Loop: This loop is optional, but can make it easier to add beads to your hair wrap. Simply take a thin piece of wire—approximately 24 gauge (.5 mm) —then bend and wrap as shown in diagram.

Diagram

Hair Divider: A hair divider is used when braiding very small sections of hair. To make the divider, cut a circle from a piece of cardstock. Mark the center of the circle and cut a thin slit from one edge to the center. Divide the hair that will be braided and wrapped from the rest of your hair, then place the hair divider against your scalp. Pull the small section of hair to be wrapped through the slit. This will keep the section free and clear from the rest of your hair, making it easier to braid and wrap only the portion that you want to.

Scrunchie or elastic: Scrunchies and elastics make great tools for hair wrapping, as they keep the unwanted hair out of the way while braiding and wrapping larger sections of hair.

HAIR WRAP INSTRUCTIONS

★ Decide on the design of the wrap you would like to create. Select the threads and embellishments you are going to use in your wrap, and place all of your materials and supplies in an easily accessible area. Find a comfortable chair of the appropriate height, and you're ready to begin!

★ Having a second person actually do the wrapping is much easier, as well as essential if the wrap is going to be at the back of the head. However, if wrapping the hair on the sides, you may be able to create the wraps yourself.

Note: You may want to practice on a piece of roving or cording before actually beginning to wrap. To make your practicing easier, select a roving that is approximately the size of the hair you will braid, wrap masking tape around each end, and then secure roving to a clip board before you begin to wrap. This will secure the base roving and the threads while wrapping. Now practice until you are comfortable with the technique and can create the desired wrap.

★ Separate the section that is to be wrapped from the rest of your hair. Place your hair divider around the braid. (Optional)

★ Measure the length of your braid. For a single-wrapped braid, multiply this length by five and cut that amount from the thread or fiber you plan to use. For a double-wrapped braid, multiply the length of the braid by ten, cut that amount from the thread or fiber you plan to use, and fold the thread in half. If you are only planning to wrap half of the braid, cut just two-and-a-half times the amount of thread.

If using single strands of thread, tie threads together with a loose knot, slip over the braid, and use a piece of floss to secure the threads at the base of the braid near the scalp.

If threads are to be doubled, take the length of the thread and fold in half. At the very center of the thread, tie a loose slip-knot and slip over the braid.

Note: The tighter and more securely you tie the knot around the braid, the longer the wrap will stay in your hair. You will want to push the knot to the top of the braid, tightening as securely as is comfortable.

When beginning your hair wrap, it is important to wrap the threads that will be used for wrapping over and over the knot at the top of the wrap. This will help secure the wrap. You should also keep pushing the threads up toward the roots of the hair as you securely wrap the threads over the knot.

Now you are ready to begin wrapping the design that you have selected. If you have chosen a design from this book, turn to that page and begin your wrap!

When ending your wrap, secure the end of the braid by wrapping with an elastic or tying with a piece of thread. If the braid is very small, hair gel might be sufficient for holding the braid together.

HOW TO MAKE A BASIC WRAP KNOT

Step 1
Using right hand, tightly hold the braid. Knot the thread around the braid.

Step 2
Pull thread to left until tight.

Step 3
Repeat.

Step 4
Finished knot for wrapping.

ATTACHING BEADS

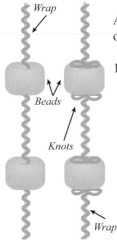

Attaching beads to hair wraps can be done in a number of ways:

1. If the hole in the bead is large enough, the bead can simply be slipped over the wrapped braid. If the bead is fairly secure, it can be left in place; however, if the hole is too large and the bead slips, it can be secured by dabbing a small amount of glue inside the hole before slipping over the wrap. Allow to dry. (Diagram 1)

An alternative to gluing the bead is to "tie" it into place by adding a small knot at both ends of the bead using a matching fiber. (Diagram 2)

Diagram 1   Diagram 2

2. If the bead hole is a tight fit, use your Beading Wire Loop. Push the loop through the selected beads, making sure the beads do not fall off. To use the Beading Wire Loop, push your right thumb and first finger through the Beading Wire Loop, just above the beads, and grab the wrap with these fingers. Pull the threads through the wire loop, pushing the beads up over the wire loop and onto the threads.

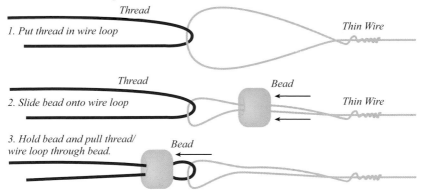

3. If the beads you want to use have a hole that is too small to fit over the wrap, you can string the beads onto a separate piece of thread or thin wire and tie this "extra embellishment" to your completed wrap.

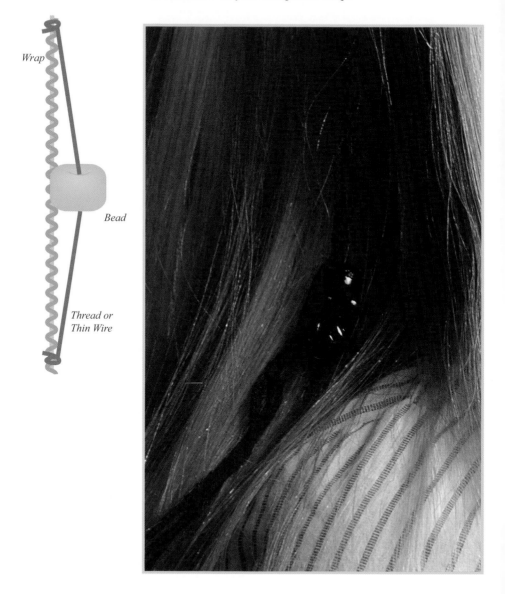

Wrap

Bead

Thread or Thin Wire

Two-Color Wraps

1. Select two colors of thread or specialty fibers, measure length of braid, measure thread 5 times the estimated length of wrap, cut two lengths of each color. (See page 36)

2. Start your hair wrap. (See pages 40-44)

3. Hold two strands of color #1 thread against braid, wrap two strands of color #2 securely over braid and thread #1. (Diagram 1)

   Wrap until desired amount of color #2 is wrapped.

4. Pick up the two strands of color #1 and wrap over braid and color #2 until desired amount of color is achieved. (Diagram 2)

5. Continue wrapping and alternating colors.

6. Finish end of wrap as desired.

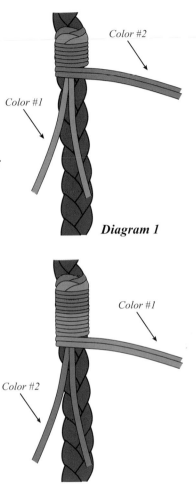

Color #2

Color #1

Diagram 1

Color #1

Color #2

Making Cross-Overs

1. Choose two colors of thread, measure ten times the estimated length of wrap, cut, and fold in half. (See page 36)

2. Start your hair wrap. (See pages 40-44)

3. Place color #2 thread against braid and wrap color #1 over braid and color #2 for about 3" (8 cm). (Diagram 1) Pull the color #2 up and out of the way and continue wrapping entire braid with color #1. (Diagram 2)

4. Cross the two threads of color #2 around the wrapped threads of color #1 to create cross-overs. (Diagram 3)

5. When you reach the end of the wrap, bring cross-over threads together, place against braid, and wrap over braid and cross-over threads with color #1 to secure. (Diagram 4)

6. End wrap as desired.

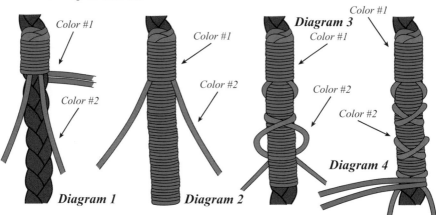

Diagram 1

Diagram 2

Diagram 3

Diagram 4

Color #1

Color #1

Color #1

Color #1

Color #2

Color #2

Color #2

Color #2

Twisted Wraps

1. Choose two colors of thread, measure ten times the estimated length of wrap, cut, and fold in half. (See page 36)

2. Start your hair wrap. (See pages 40-44)

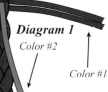

3. Place color #2 thread against braid and wrap color #1 over braid and color #2 for about 2" (5 cm). (Diagram 1) Pull the color #2 up and out of the way and continue wrapping entire braid with color #1. (Diagram 2)

Diagram 1

Color #2

Color #1

4. Twist the 2 threads of color #2 together tightly to form a spiral. Wrap the spiral down the braid around color #1. (Diagrams 3-4)

5. When you reach the end of the wrap, tie the spiral threads securely around the end of the braid and wrap with color #1.

6. End wrap as desired.

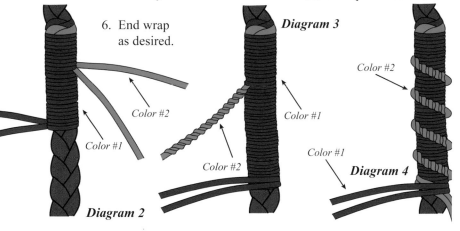

Diagram 3

Color #2

Color #1

Color #2

Color #1

Color #2

Color #1

Diagram 4

Diagram 2

Fancy Feet

A Treat
For Your Feet

by Heather Hammonds

Beautiful Feet

Hey girls, let's stop and look down for a moment. Yes, let's take a look at those feet!

Every day we walk, run and stand on them for hours. They deserve your attention.

Beautiful feet, like beautiful hands, can really get you noticed. So, as well as taking care of your hands and fingernails, you should spare some time for your tootsies. Pamper them with soothing pedicures and foot massages after a hard day of walking around. Brighten them up with the enormous range of decorations available today for your feet and nails. And most of all … show them off!

Summertime and parties are the times when beautiful feet and toenails really come into their own. Whether you're wearing sandals or flip-flops or just walking barefoot on the beach, sparkling toenails, unique foot art and trendy toe rings are sure to catch everyone's eye.

So where can you get some great tips to brighten up your tootsies? Right here! In the following pages you will find lots of information on how to care for your feet. You'll also find pages of exciting ideas on how to get that perfect look for everyday wear or special occasions.

Fancy feet are fun and glamorous, so turn the page, read on and have fun!

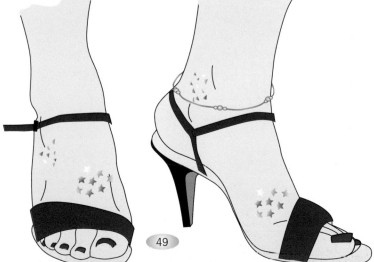

Polish and Preen

Nail Polish

What better way to show off your toenails than to make them shimmer and shine with a brilliant coat of nail polish.

Nail polish comes in a huge range of colors and types.

- Pearl polishes have a smooth, pale sheen similar to real pearls.

- Gloss polishes have a highly reflective, glossy finish.

- Matt polishes are less shiny and usually come in bold colors.

- Luminous polishes come in bold, glowing fluorescent colors.

- Chrome polishes come in fabulous metallic colors.

Polish and Preen

Application

First, use a toe separator to separate your toes.

Apply a coat of nail strengthener to your toenails. Allow to dry. Nail strengthener will help protect your toenails from chipping or breaking.

Now apply a thin layer of base coat. Base coat will stop any color in the nail polish from staining your nails. Allow to dry.

Apply the nail polish of your choice to each toenail. Allow to dry.

Finish off by painting a layer of glossy top coat over your toe-nails, to give them a brilliant shine.

Tip!

Silver and gold chrome polishes look stunning. Use them when you're wearing sandals with silver or gold buckles.

Rings 'n' Things

There are many fabulous ways to decorate your feet and toes. You can use them in combination with nail polish to create just the right effect for that perfect night out or a fun party look.

Toe Rings

Toe rings are very popular in India, and they are a symbol of love. Some Indian women wear silver toe rings that were placed on their toes by their husbands during their marriage ceremony. Sometimes, toe rings are connected by decorative chains to anklets. Today, toe rings are so beautiful that women all over the world wear them whether they are married or not.

Just like finger rings, toe rings come in many different designs. Some are simple and inexpensive while others are made of precious metals like gold or silver and are studded with valuable stones.

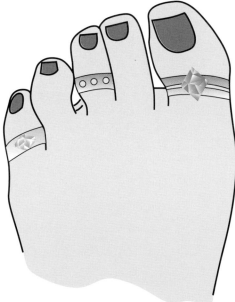

Rings 'n' Things

Anklets

Anklets, or ankle bracelets, are also worn by many women in India and all around the world. They may be simple, fine chains or they may be decorated with bells or charms. You can create your own anklets—we'll show you how later in this book.

Temporary Tattoos

Temporary tattoos look fantastic on your feet and come in a huge range of designs, from flowers to animals and novelty cartoon characters. Temporary tattoos are available from beauty shops, novelty shops and drugstores.

The great thing about temporary tattoos is that you can wash them off when you get tired of them and want to change your look. When buying them, be sure to find ones that are easily removed with soap and water. Then Mom won't mind when she sees you wearing them.

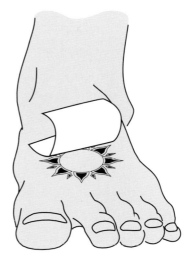

Rings 'n' Things

Tattoo Pens and Stamps

Temporary tattoo pens and stamps can be bought in the same places as temporary tattoos, and they come in a wide range of exciting colors.

You can use tattoo pens to create exotic foot art to match your nail polish designs or your toe rings and anklets. You can also try creating some more traditional foot art designs, like those used in the exotic Indian art of mehndi.

Tip!

You can combine temporary tattoos with your own designs, drawn on with tattoo pens to create an individual look that everyone will admire!

Stick-On Fun

Stick-on decorations are another fantastic way to dress up your feet and toenails. You can buy inexpensive stick-on decorations from places such as drugstores, beauty shops and craft shops, and even over the Internet.

Nail Stickers

Nail stickers are small stickers made especially for your fingernails and toenails. They come in packs of ten (for ten fingers or toes) and are used by professional nail artists around the world. Nail stickers are easy to apply because they are self-adhesive, so all you have to do is peel off the backing and stick them right onto your toenails. They come in many designs, from pretty flowers through to cartoon characters. The choice is yours!

Stick-On Jewels

Stick-on jewels are one of the hottest fashion accessories available today. Just like regular nail stickers they come in sets of ten and range from brilliant imitation diamonds to red rubies, green emeralds and many other colors. Stick them on your toenails after applying polish, or try sticking them to your ankles or toes. Most are self-adhesive and you simply peel the backing off and stick them on.

The Four Seasons

* You can give yourself a different look for each season that all your friends will admire!

Spring Surprises

Spring is the time for flowers. Glam up your feet with some sparkling daisies for this super season.

You will need:

- Base coat
- Small round, yellow stick-on jewels
- Pink and white nail polishes
- Fine craft brush (available from craft stores)
- Top coat
- Temporary tattoo pen

1. Paint a base coat on your toenails. Allow to dry. Then paint on the pink polish. Allow to dry.

2. Carefully stick a yellow jewel in the center of each toenail.

3. Using the craft brush, create a daisy on each toenail by painting petals around each jewel with white polish. Allow to dry.

Tip!

It's a good idea to practice drawing your tattoo designs on a sheet of paper first.

4. Apply a glossy top coat around the jewels, and allow to dry.

5. To complete your springtime look, use the tattoo pen to draw a chain of small daisies from the nail on each big toe up and around each ankle.

Summer Sizzlers

Get a cool look for summer with stunning sunshine toenails, exotic foot art and beautiful toe rings, too!

You will need:

- Base coat
- Bright blue and yellow nail polishes (luminous colors are ideal)
- Fine craft brush
- Top coat
- Temporary tattoo pen
- Toe rings (optional)

1. Paint a base coat on your toenails. Allow to dry. Then paint on a coat of bright blue polish. Allow to dry.

2. Using the craft brush, carefully paint a small sun on each of your toenails with the yellow polish. Allow to dry.

3. Apply a top coat for a glossy finish. Allow to dry.

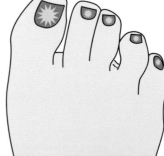

4. Now use the tattoo pen to draw a beautiful sun on the center of each of your feet. Give your suns an exotic flame look. You could even give them a face.

5. Place a toe ring on each of your feet, if you wish. Alternatively, create 'rings' on each toe with the tattoo pen.

Amazing Autumn

Autumn is the time to get out your rich red and brown polishes, to match the falling leaves.

You will need:

- Base coat
- Rich, deep red and brown nail polishes
- Top coat
- Red stick-on jewels (any shape) or autumn-leaf-shaped stickers
- Temporary tattoo pen (optional)

Tip!

Temporary tattoos can also be used with most designs, in place of a tattoo pen. When shopping, keep an eye out for them and start a collection. Then, when you are dressing up your feet, you will have something in your collection that is just right for every occasion.

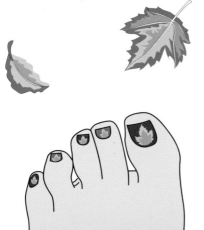

The Four Seasons

1. Paint a base coat on your toenails. Allow to dry. Then alternately paint your toenails rich red and brown. Allow to dry.

2. Paint on a glossy top coat. Allow to dry.

3. Place a jewel or sticker in the center of each of your toenails—but don't stop there. For added effect, place an extra jewel or sticker at the base of each toe.

4. If you wish, you can now add to this stunning autumn effect by drawing a line of autumn leaves around each ankle.

Wild Winter

Winter is the coldest time of the year, but your tootsies can still be Hot! Hot! Hot! Be bold and try out this striking stormy design.

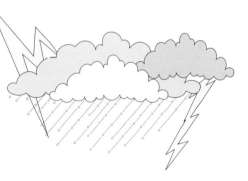

You will need:

- Base coat
- Black nail polish and bright yellow polish (luminous yellow is best)
- Fine craft brush
- Clear glitter polish (optional)
- Tattoo pen

The Four Seasons

1. Paint a base coat on your toenails. Allow to dry. Then paint on a coat of black polish. Allow to dry.

2. Using the craft brush, carefully paint a bold zigzag lightning bolt of yellow polish down each of your toenails. Allow to dry.

3. If you wish, you can now paint on an extra coat of glitter polish instead of regular top coat. Glitter polishes are clear gloss polishes with different colored glitter mixed through them. We recommend gold glitter for this design. Allow to dry.

4. To complete your stormy look, draw a lightning bolt on the outside of each of your ankles, stretching down from your ankle bone to the base of your toes.

Wild!

Retro Look

Let's take a trip back in time to the 1960s and dress up your feet and nails with some retro fashion. The following two designs are fantastic when worn in the summertime with your best faded jeans, sandals and a wide-brimmed sunhat.

Psychedelic Swirl

You'll love this unusual multicolored design!

You will need:

- Base coat
- Bright yellow nail polish
- Red, green and blue nail polishes
- Fine craft brush
- Top coat
- Selection of colored stick-on jewels

1. Paint a base coat on your toenails. Allow to dry. Then paint on a coat of yellow polish. Allow to dry.

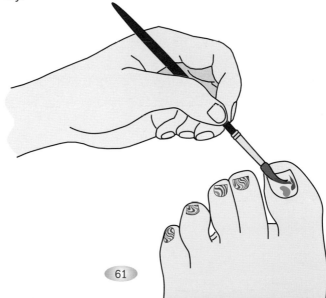

Retro Look

2. Carefully place a very small drop of red, green and blue polish on each toenail. Then use the craft brush to stir the colors together in a swirling motion. Don't stir too much—just enough to mix the colors in a circular pattern. Allow to dry.

3. Paint on a glossy top coat. Allow to dry.

4. Now stick a colored jewel on the base of each of your toes for a far-out, dazzling effect!

Flower Power

Traditional flower designs were all the rage in the sixties—and they still are!

You will need:

- Base coat
- Light green and bright orange nail polishes
- Fine craft brush

Retro Look

1. Paint a base coat on your toenails. Allow to dry. Then apply a coat of light green polish. Allow to dry.

2. Using the craft brush, place a small dot of orange polish in the center of each toenail. Then very carefully paint orange petals around each dot of polish to create some way-out flowers. Allow to dry.

3. Paint on a glossy top coat. Allow to dry.

4. Now draw some fabulous flowers around each ankle and down the center of each foot with the tattoo pen. Alternatively, stick on some groovy flower stickers. Your glamorous flowery look will have all your friends admiring your fancy feet.

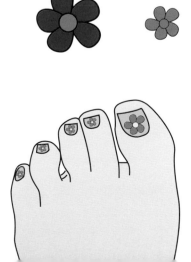

Tip!

Try using different colored polishes with these retro designs, too.

Star Treatment

Girls, these are definitely the greatest looks for those formal nights out where you want to shine. They're glitzy, glamorous and go beautifully with that pair of high heels you keep for special occasions.

Shimmering Stars

Stars look brilliant on the feet. Try this stunning design.

You will need:

- Base coat
- Gold and silver chrome polishes
- Fine craft brush
- Top coat
- Silver star stickers or clear star-shaped stick-on jewels

1. Paint a base coat on your toenails. Allow to dry. Then paint on a coat of gold polish. Allow to dry.

2. Now use the fine craft brush to paint on some twinkling stars with the silver polish. Allow to dry.

3. Apply a glossy top coat. Allow to dry.

Tip!

Change the placement of your star stickers or jewels, depending on the design of your shoes. Sometimes they will have a greater effect if placed around your ankles.

Star Treatment

4. Finally, place a line of silver star stickers or stick-on jewels in a line down the center of each foot to the base of your middle toe. Now you're ready to put those high heels on to finish the formal effect!

Swirling Galaxies

The universe is full of sparkling, swirling galaxies—so put some on your toenails!

You will need:

- Base coat
- Black gloss and silver chrome nail polishes
- Toothpick or fine craft brush
- Top coat
- Temporary tattoo pen

1. Paint a base coat on your toenails. Allow to dry. Then paint on a coat of black polish. Allow to dry.

2. Now dip the toothpick or the wooden end of the craft brush in the silver polish. Carefully apply lots of tiny little dots (these are the stars) to each toe in a swirling, galaxy pattern. Apply only a tiny dot of polish for each star in the galaxy so the dots do not run together. Allow to dry.

Star Treatment

3. Apply a glossy top coat. Allow to dry.

4. Use your tattoo pen to draw a small star at the base of each toe. Then draw a half moon around the outside ankle bone and the inside ankle bone of each foot to complete an unusual look that will catch everyone's attention.

Feline Feet

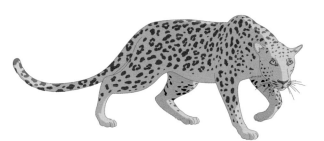

With these designs from big and small cats, you can give yourself a 'purrfect' feline look. So paint them on and have some fun!

You will need:

- Base coat
- Yellow and dark brown nail polishes
- Fine craft brush
- Top coat

1. Paint a base coat on your toenails. Allow to dry. Then paint on a coat of yellow polish. Allow to dry.

2. Now use the craft brush to paint on lots of little leopard spots with the dark brown polish. Allow to dry.

Tip!

This design looks great with gold-colored foot jewelry, so put on any golden toe rings or anklets you have, to complete this wild look.

Feline Feet

3. Paint a base coat on your toenails. Allow to dry. Then paint on a coat of yellow polish. Allow to dry.

Now use the craft brush to paint on lots of little leopard spots with the dark brown polish. Allow to dry.

Tortoiseshell Toes

Did you know that tortoiseshell cats are always female? It's true! They are also known for being intelligent, elegant creatures, with a style all their own.

You will need:

- Base coat
- Dark brown, light brown, yel-low and orange nail polishes
- Fine craft brush
- Top coat

1. Paint a base coat on your toenails. Allow to dry. Then paint on a layer of dark brown nail polish. Allow to dry.

Feline Feet

2. Using the fine craft brush, paint a layer of spots on each toenail with the yellow polish. Allow to dry.

3. Repeat step 2 with the light brown and orange nail polishes. Allow to dry each time. Build up the layers of polish until you have a mottled, tortoiseshell look.

4. Finally, paint on a glossy top coat. Allow to dry.

Your Own Designs

Below you will find some beautiful patterns that you can use to decorate your toes, feet and ankles. We also suggest that you create some of your own designs and keep a scrapbook for this purpose. Then, when you see one of your favorite celebrities wearing beautiful foot decorations, you can cut the picture out or copy the design. Stick it into your scrapbook for later use.

Let's Make Clothespin Dolls

Text and Designs by
Rafaella Dowling and Jessica Dowling

Photography by F. William Lagaret

Introduction

In the days before department stores and mass merchandisers were readily accessible, children used their imaginations to devise entertaining games and toys. Children then as now proved to be creative and resourceful. The making of clothespin dolls was one such invention that remains as much fun today as before. Using scraps of fabric, paper and ribbon, children were able to transform ordinary clothespins into extraordinary dolls.

The materials you need to make clothespin dolls are easy to find. They're more than likely around your house right now. In a world where most toys need batteries to operate, what better way to tap into your own creativity than to take part in a wonderful pastime like making clothespin dolls.

The Basics

To make clothespin dolls, simply use scissors and glue to transform scraps of material into tiny bits of clothing. The ease in making clothes for these dolls is that they do not need elaborate hems or joints like clothes for people. You can simply configure scraps in a way that you like to create outfits for your dolls, using glue to hold them in place.

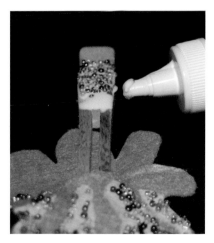
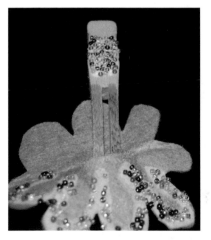

Suggested Materials

Keep in mind that you don't need to use all of these. You can also come up with other creative things to use. Look around. You're sure to be inspired.

- Plain Clothespins
- Markers
- Gel Pens
- Fabric Paints (Puffy Paint)
- Glitter
- Felt or other scrap fabric
- Colored Paper

- Sequins
- Seed Beads
- Ribbon
- Yarn
- Stickers
- Glue

Tips

Creating Faces:

You can draw a face directly on your clothespin doll or draw a face on a small round binder sticker and stick it on your doll.

Making Yarn Hair:

To make yarn hair, make a peace sign (V-sign with your middle and index fingers) and loop yarn several times around your two fingers. In the middle of this yarn, tightly tie a smaller piece of yarn. Then, cut the ends of the loops. You now have a yarn "wig" that you can glue to your clothespin doll's head. Experiment with different yarn lengths and colors until you give your doll the perfect head of hair!

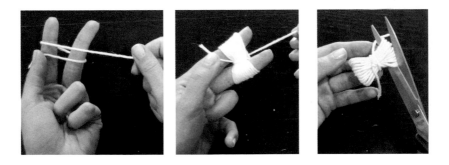

Yarn Wrapping:

Wrap yarn around the clothespin to create dresses, shirts or pants. This technique makes a great clothing base to later decorate with glitter or sequins.

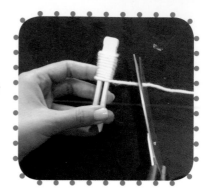

Making Paper Clothes:

Make a pencil outline of a clothespin on colored paper. Using this as a template, create a paper outfit that will fit your doll. Decorate with glitter, sequins, markers— anything you like! When you are done, carefully cut out the outfit and glue it to your doll.

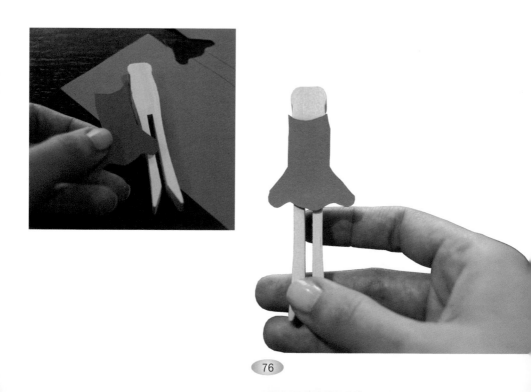

Making Fabric Clothing:

An easy way to make a dress is to wrap a rectangular piece of fabric around your clothespin doll. Add a yarn "belt" to tie it in place and proceed to decorate. You'll have a sophisticated strapless dress in no time, with no glue!

Adding Fancy Fringe:

To create a sophisticated fringe on the hem of a doll's dress or skirt, cut small slits in the bottom of the paper/fabric and gently separate.

Remember:
To prevent a sticky mess, be patient and wait for glue to dry before adding another "layer" of clothing or before decorating fabric or paper you have glued on. You won't have to wait long because ordinary glue takes no time to dry.

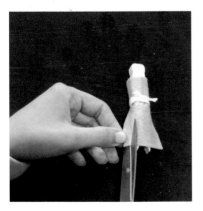
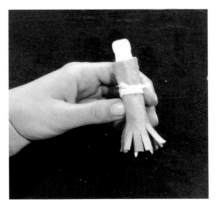

Making Arms:

To create simple arms for your clothespin doll, cut two small lengths of yarn. Tie a knot at the end of each one to make "hands." Now, trim the length of yarn so the arms are proportionate to your doll. Simply glue the yarn pieces to either side of the doll's torso.

Making Shoes:

To make simple shoes, you can cut a small piece of ribbon at a 45 degree angle for each shoe and glue it to the foot of your clothespin doll. Alternately, you can draw the shoes on with marker. For fun "slippers," try gluing a brightly colored mini pom-pom to each foot!

Since you'll have many tiny pieces of fabric, yarn and paper after making these dolls, it's a good idea to keep a special box for them (an empty shoe box with a lid would be fine). Fill this box with the materials you need so you will always have them at hand when you want to make clothes-would be fine). Fill this box with the materials you need so you will always have them at hand when you want to make clothes-pin dolls. The box will keep the scraps organized, and they won't clutter up your house!

Remember:
Don't forget to save scraps of pretty paper and fabric from other projects to make clothes for your dolls! Even a tiny scrap of fabric can make a beautiful gown when it's for a clothespin!

Ways to use clothespin dolls:

- Make into Christmas ornaments.

- Make sports-themed dolls and give one to each player on your team.

- Decorate an empty shoebox with markers and glitter, and use it as a dollhouse for your clothespin dolls.

- Make a clothespin doll to represent each member of your family.

- Make clothespin dolls of your pets.

Most of all, have fun!

Sporty Fun!

Splashy

Mermaids

Princess

Pageant!

Fantasy

Fairies!

Ballerina

Beauties!

Feathered

Friends

Painting on Rocks

Illustrated by Raffaella, Jessica, and Devon Dowling

Text by Jessica Dowling

Photography by F. William Lagaret

Painting Animals on Rocks

Illustrated by
Rafaella and Jessica Dowling

Text by Jessica Dowling

Photography by F. William Lagaret

Why Paint Rocks?

Rock painting is an easy and inexpensive way to create your own art! Painting rocks allows you to use your creativity in ways different than when you paint on paper or canvas. By studying the shape of the rock you can imagine all sorts of things that the rock could become.

What can I do with painted rocks?

Painted rocks make unique and expressive indoor or out- door decorations. Put them on your mantle,

your nightstand, or even use larger ones for bookends. They are great patio decorations, and a few tucked in a flowerpot always look pretty. Don't forget: painted rocks make wonderful gifts, too!

I don't know how to paint!

Rock painting is the perfect medium for beginners. If you mess up, just prime the rock over again and start out fresh. In addition, since the shape of the rock often suggests a form, it is easier for the beginning artist to pick a subject. Painting rocks is great for advanced  artists, too! Challenge yourself and see how detailed your rocks can become.

When someone mistakenly bites into a rock you've painted to look like a cookie, you're an expert!

What do I paint on a rock?

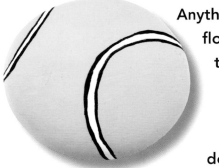 Anything! Paint your favorite animal or flower, or create a rock with a sports theme. Paint a letter on each of several rocks, and spell out your name or that of a friend. Paint vegetables or fruits on rocks to decorate a kitchen, or different sea creatures to decorate a bathroom. An apple-painted rock given to a teacher will last much longer than the real thing! The possibilities of what to paint are absolutely endless. Use your imagination!

Where can I find rocks?

Most arts and crafts stores sell smooth polished river
stones. These have mostly round or oblong shapes;
so if you want to find more unique rocks, get outside!
Many rocks of varying shapes, sizes and textures can
be found at the beach, or near rivers and lakes. If you
live in a city, you can try looking for rocks in a park.
Always make sure to have an
adult with you when
you go out looking
for rocks.

Priming

Because rocks are often dark or bumpy, it is important
to prime them before you paint your design. This pre-
pares the rock to be painted on. To prime a rock, simply cover it with a thick coat of white paint and allow
it to dry completely. It's okay if the rock's color still
shows through; it will get covered up when you paint
your design.

Materials

Acrylic Paint. A good basic set of paints would consist of white, black, red, blue, and yellow. You can mix most other colors you might want to use from these. You may, however, wish to invest in some extra paints since colors such as magenta and brown may be difficult to mix on your own. You'll find two-ounce bottles of acrylic craft paint are fairly inexpensive. They work great and cost much less than fine arts acrylics.

Acrylic brushes in several sizes. Consider starting out with a size 6 filbert, a size 4 round, and a size 0 round (for fine details). Try out different brush sizes as you determine your artistic needs.

Clear acrylic glaze to protect rocks that are displayed outside or to give your indoor rocks a brilliant sheen. This glaze comes in aerosol cans or in liquid form to be painted on. Use the liquid form for painting rocks because it adheres better, and you can apply it indoors. A small bottle (around 120 ml) should last a long time.

Toothpicks. These are great for painting tiny details or dots.

A cup of water to clean brushes.

Paper towels for surface cleanup.

Newspaper to lay on top of your work area and protect surfaces.

A pencil to sketch out your design on the rock. A soft pencil works best, as it will show up on the rock better. Instead of a standard #2 pencil, pick up a soft 6B pencil at an art supply store.

Scrap paper to jot down ideas. Always keep some paper with you in case a great idea for a painted rock strikes you when you are on the go!

Animal Rocks

Whale

Octopus

Crab

Fish

Cat

If you'd like, sketch a loose design on a primed rock with a soft pencil before you start painting.

Owl

Sleeping Cat

Eagle

Bee

Dinosaur

Bunny

Yummy Rocks

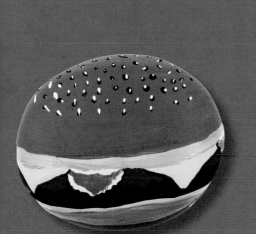

Cheeseburger

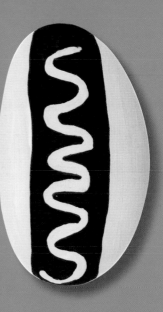

Hot Dog

Pizza

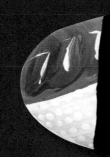

Sushi

TIP!

A little paint goes a long way! Put only a dab of each color on your palette, you can always add more.

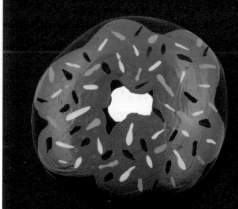

Donut

Pot of tea

Cup of tea

Cupcake

Cookie

The colors of your design will be clearer and more vibrant if you do a good job priming the rock first.

Cherries

nature
Rocks

Sun

Rainbow

Mountains

Desert

Fluffy Clouds

TIP!

Experiment using a thin permanent marker on finished, totally dry rocks. Use it to outline objects, or add fine details.

Sunrise

Beach

Moon

Rain Cloud

Change the water you use to clean your brushes often, to prevent muddy colors.

Volcano

Painted rocks make great paperweights or doorstoppers!

Sunflower

Tulip

Rose

Daisies

Daffodil

Wildflowers

Use two or more painted rocks to create a composition. For instance, a rock with a tree painted on it, one with a bench, and one with a fountain make an adorable park!

Rock
Designs

Circles and Lines

Tiny Dots

Curly Lines

Lots of Circles

Criss Cross

Swirls and Stripes

Toothpicks are one of the most useful tools for painting rocks. Dipping one in a small amount of paint allows you to create fine details and designs.

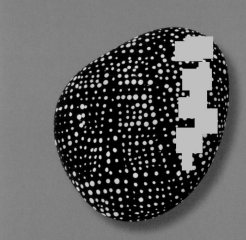

Dot Pattern

Checkerboard

TIP!

Good lighting conditions are key! Make sure you are working in bright light. This will allow you to see colors clearly, and keep your eyes from working too hard.

Bright Stripes

Happy Stripes

Cat Rocks

If rocks are dirty or muddy, wash them with warm water and dish soap, then pat dry with paper towels.

Puppy Rocks

If you'd like, sketch a loose design on a primed rock with a soft pencil before you start painting.

Bird Rocks

Make sure to take a break from painting every so often to give your hands and eyes a rest.

Bug Rocks

A little paint goes a long way! Put only a dab of each color on your palette, you can always add more.

Barnyard Rocks

Try to think of creative backgrounds for your subject matter. Don't always use white! Try bright colors, stripes, or even polka dots as a backdrop for your creations.

Jungle Rocks

To make rocks more brilliant, give them a coat of clear acrylic after they are completely dry.

For Further Fun

The material in this book has been selected from the following Mud Puddle Books publications:

Beaded Friendship Bracelets by Kaylee Connor, copyright © 2007, Mud Puddle Books; part of *Beaded Friendship Bracelets: Book & Kit.*

Hair Wraps: All the Fun Things You Need to Know for Easy and Beautiful Hair Decoration by Jo Packham, copyright © 2007; part of *Hair Wraps: Book & Kit.*

Fancy Feet: A Treat for Your Feet! by Heather Hammonds, copyright © 2003, Hinkler Books Pty Ltd (17-23 Redwood Drive, Dingley Victoria 3172 Australia); part of *Fancy Feet Book & Kit.*

Let's Make Clothespin Dolls text and designs by Raffaella Dowling & Jessica Dowling and photographs by F. William Lagaret, copyright © 2008, Mud Puddle Books; part of *Clothespin Dolls: Book & Kit.*

Painting on Rocks illustrated by Raffaella, Jessica & Devin Dowling, text by Jessica Dowling and photography by F. William Lagaret, copyright © 2006, Mud Puddle Books; part of *Rock Painting: Book & Kit.*

Painting Animals on Rocks illustrated by Raffaella & Jessica Dowling, text by Jessica Dowling and photography by F. William Lagaret, copyright © 2008, Mud Puddle Books; part of *Painting Animals on Rocks: Book & Kit.*

Continue your fun! Look for these and other Mud Puddle titles.